❧FAIRY HOUSE❧
COOKING

❦ FAIRY HOUSE ❧
COOKING

Simple Scrumptious Recipes
& Fairy Party Fun!

LIZA GARDNER WALSH

Down East Books

Published by Down East Books
An imprint of Globe Pequot

Distributed by National Book Network

Photographs by Andrew Dumas, Cross Street Photography, except: Ben Magro pgs. 7 middle, 8, 72, 110-111; Phoebe Walsh pgs. 6 middle, 7 bottom, 29, 41, 45, 51, 56, 58, 59, 100, 102, 105; Lynda Chilton pgs. 6 bottom, 28, 55, 57, 74-inset, 80; Jess Chamberlain p. 52; blickwinkel / Alamy Stock Photo p. 103; istock photos: SolStock p. 2, Milanchikov p. 43, Geo-grafika p. 65, Donna Coleman p. 74, SherSor p. 75, ratmaner p. 77 left, Supapich_Garcia p. 77 right, Christopher Futcher p. 79, domin_domin p. 81, Yulia_Davidovich p. 83, TransientEternal p. 84, mtreasure p. 86, Diane Labombarbe p. 87, NatashaPhoto p. 89, bonchan p. 91, Francisco Romero p. 92, FerhatMatt p. 96, kurapy11 p. 98, PeopleImages p. 99, projectspawn p. 104; Dreamstime photos: Nqrdigital p. 3, Blair_witch p. 9, Qwartm p. 29, Schmaelterphoto p. 37, Floortje p. 57, pumpkin-Milllda p. 59, Elenathewise p. 63, Winnietam p. 70; Janet Hudson p. 53; Mene Tekel p. 55; Aftabbanoori p. 65, fourth inset from top; Stan Shebs p. 65, third inset from top; Jörg Hempel p. 65, secont image from top at right; Captain-tucker p. 64 bottom inset; Hans Bernhard p. 64 top inset

Designed by Lynda Chilton, Chilton Creative

British Library Cataloging in Publication Information Available

Library of Congress Cataloging-in-Publication Data Available

ISBN 978-1-60893-641-0 (cloth : alk. paper)
ISBN 978-1-68475-119-8 (paper : alk. paper)
ISBN 978-1-60893-652-6 (electronic)

♾™ The paper used in this publication meets or exceeds the minimum requirements of American National Standard for Information Sciences—Permanence of Paper for Printed Library Materials, ANSI/NISO
Z39.48-1992

To my grandmother, Mary Gardner,
my first baking teacher who always
baked with love.

Table of Contents

INTRODUCTION

"There is mystery in cooking; no matter how many times you make the same dish, it will never be the exact same."

— Marion Cunningham

Welcome to the kitchen! Whether your cooking experience only goes as far as adding milk to cereal or you are training to be a star on a cooking show, perhaps you already have a sense that this place is filled with magic, mystery, and lots of messy fun. Cooking is obviously about creating things to eat, but aside from adding real, actual ingredients, cooking also gives you a set of skills that you can't see with your eyes. Kind of like the way

you can't always see fairies but you know they are near.

First, you have to be **creative** to picture how a bunch of powders and liquids can mix together to turn into something yummy and beautiful. You have to be **flexible** when things go wrong. **Resourceful** when you need to substitute a different ingredient. **Patient** when those cookies are taking way longer than they were supposed to. And **cooperative** when you need to take turns with your younger sister or brother. It will even help you become a better **reader** and **mathematician**. Cooking also makes you more **appreciative** of the food around you, the meals served, the vegetables in your garden, as well as the groceries at the store. And at its heart, cooking is about **nourishment**, a big word for a happy belly and a growing body.

Some of my favorite cooking was done in my backyard when I was growing up, grass clippings, flower blossoms, and pine cones. These "fairy soups" were my first adventure into putting lots of stuff into a pot to see what would happen. Sometimes the concoctions looked beautiful and sometimes they were disgusting. I soon came to find out that cooking in the kitchen was very similar.

Sometimes when you cook, things fall apart. Sometimes nothing works and a hot mess emerges. You spill the milk and cry over it. Sometimes you leave something in the oven too long and it becomes like a brick. But other times, it is as if the kitchen fairies have given your recipe wings and you pull out the tastiest cake ever made. This is when cooking feels magical. There is joy in cooking and there is hard work, plus a lot of mess and a lot of cleaning up. Like most things, it takes practice. And since cooking is most likely something you will do your whole life—maybe even three times a day—it is a good idea to have fun with it.

Cooking with the fairies in mind does just that. Fairies approach cooking with a festive spirit. They love gathering around a table and sharing nature's bounty. They also love honey, cakes, milk, and edible flowers. This book is for fairy lovers. It is for the friends of the fairies. It is for kids planning parties and spending aimless days collecting flowers in gardens to create a backyard feast. It is a book that has treats, both healthy ones and some that are for special occasions, and simple activities that don't even require a stove. Most of these recipes are for you to eat, some are for the fairies or your pet bunny or your stuffed animals. It is part cookbook, part nature cookbook, and part party planner. This is NOT a book about cooking fairies, that would just be mean!

But please note, this is also not a book that will help you make dinner for your family on a Tuesday night after soccer practice. It is filled with a fair amount of 'special occasion' food. What I, and most grownups, refer to as treats. Even though you may disagree, you don't *need* a cookie a day. So pull this book out when you have friends coming over, or your grandparents are arriving, or it is May Day, or when it has been a week filled with tons of spinach.

DIFFICULTY LEVELS

Some of these recipes are easy. For others, you will need a grown-up to help you. With each recipe there is a difficulty scale.

One fairy wing means, you got this. It is like doing something with the hand that you write with—comfortable.

Two wings mean that a grown-up should be in the room, providing some guidance or moral support.

Three wings mean that this is a true team effort, you will really need a grown-up's help.

COOKING TIPS

⚙ WASH YOUR HANDS!!! And not just a quick rinse. Really soap them up, wash the backs of your hands, under your nails, and between your fingers.

⚙ Make sure there is an adult at home who knows what you are up to and can help gather ingredients and figure the recipes out.

⚙ Read the recipe from start to finish. Make sure you have everything you need and understand the steps.

⚙ Which brings us to time . . . take lots of time. Don't rush because that is when mistakes happen. It is also not safe. When you slow down it encourages you to pay attention. Make sure you have enough time to complete the recipe.

⚙ Open all of your senses. Cooking uses all of them! Taste, touch, smell, sight. Notice when something smells burnt, when the dough tastes too salty or looks too runny.

⚙ Setting up is very important. Having everything you need in front of you makes for a more enjoyable and relaxed cooking experience. Gather the supplies and measure the amount of each ingredient ahead of time.

⚙ Make sure you have a stable step stool that is easy to move. It is important to be at the right height so that everything is in reach and at eye level.

⚙ When using dry goods like flour and sugar, don't pour them out into your measuring cup. It is easier (and less messy) to dip your measuring cup into the bag.

⚙ Always opt for a bigger bowl when possible. Ingredients can fly when stirring gets really active.

CLEANING UP

I like to clean as I go. There is nothing more disheartening than pulling out a delicious cake and then looking at a sink piled with dirty dishes. My grandmother used to say that the sign of a good cook is how clean the kitchen is when they finish. As you complete parts of the recipe, continue to keep your work surface clear by putting things back in the refrigerator and placing wrappers and peelings in the trash. Wipe down the area with a clean sponge occasionally. I like to have a big sink full of warm soapy water to soak dishes in as they are used. Added bonus—the more you clean, the more your family will encourage you to cook.

One last thing: It is okay to make mistakes. I cannot tell you how many times I have used a tablespoon of something that only needed a teaspoon. Or forgot to put in eggs or used a different kind of flour. It was not the end of the world. Now, I simply double-check and go slowly, especially when adding things like baking powder and salt!

A WORD ABOUT SAFETY

Spills, knives, hot ovens—oh my! The kitchen does have its dangerous elements. But if you pay attention, have an adult on hand, and know the rules, safety will prevail.

- ☼ If you spill anything or drop something (especially a banana peel!), wipe it up immediately so no one slips.

- ☼ Be careful with sharp knives. When you are using them, keep your fingers away from the knife's edge.

- ☼ NEVER touch an electrical outlet to plug something in with wet hands. You can get a big shock.

- ☼ If you have to stand on a stool or chair to reach something, make sure it is level and sturdy.

- ☼ When cooking with a pot on a stove-top, turn the handle to the side of the stove so it can't be tipped.

- ☼ Make sure you turn off the stove as soon as you are finished using it.

ALLERGIES

Fairies are known to be quite allergic to iron and do not like the plant called St. John's Wort. If you suffer from food allergies, take heart that the fairies share your plight. There are only a few recipes in here that use nuts and each one is noted with an allergy warning. If you are gluten free, then most of the baked items will work with a gluten-free flour mix.

I have been cooking with my daughters since they were very young. It is not always easy. Sometimes they fight over who gets to add certain ingredients or they crack entire egg shells into perfectly prepared dough. Often things are burned, spilled, or misread. And every now and again mommy loses it a little. But then there are times when we make something delicious and we can't believe we did it, or we make up a recipe and it becomes our favorite meal. And, nearly every time, the kitchen gets turned upside down and we spend as long cleaning up as we did cooking. But each time it gets easier and more fun. I believe in making beautiful messes, but I also know that most of the mistakes or frustrations are a result of me not explaining things properly.

So my most serious advice is to spend a little time giving your kids a kitchen shake down. Teach them how to hold a knife safely, how to turn the oven on and off, how burners stay hot for a while even after the dial is turned off. Show them how to properly clean a bowl and how to load the dishwasher. You might even want to make a list of safety rules for your kitchen. Be specific about what they are allowed to do on their own and what they should get your help with. Charles Johnson said that "specificity is generosity," and I think this holds very true with communicating well as a parent.

Before your kids start, make sure they have washed their hands, have gone through the recipe, and have everything they need. Then take a step back. As Mollie Katzen, cookbook author extraordinaire says, "help, but don't hover." Let your kids make mistakes on occasion so they learn from them. Not everything has to be a delicious masterpiece. But by letting them explore they will soon go to the kitchen as a refuge. As Marion Cunningham describes, "When you feel troubled, there is nothing that can absorb your attention and lift your spirits like going into the kitchen, washing your hands, and starting to cook or bake. And there is nothing like the deep sense of accomplishment you will have when you share the food you've cooked with your family and friends."

FAIRY MORNINGS

One of the best ways to start the day is to check on your fairy house to see if the fairies left a treat or if there are any signs of visitation such as footprints or notes. But after this important investigation, it is time to make a special breakfast. For if you are planning on spending a day building fairy houses, then you need a good breakfast to give you fuel. This section focuses on getting your day started with the fairies by making good healthy breakfasts as well as festive ones to begin a magical day because everything is better with a full stomach. Every single recipe in this section can be adapted according to you, your tastes, and what you have on hand. If you have whole wheat flour, fine. Apples and no blueberries, fine. The key is you don't need a box of pancake mix to make pancakes, or a box of muffin mix to make muffins unless you want to use one. These recipes are remarkably easy and forgiving once you get them in your back pocket, which is another way of saying you know them by heart. So put on your apron and get ready to greet the day. The fairies are waiting for you.

Fairy Muffins

This is a no-fail, standard muffin recipe adapted from The Baker's Café, the bakery I used to go to in my town growing up. It gives you a blank canvas for creating muffins, which is really the best thing to have.

Certain muffin combinations will appeal to certain types of fairies. Any kind of berry muffin will appeal to the berry fairies. The job of the berry fairies is to watch over the ripening of all berries and they are extra busy in late summer and early fall. They are cousins of the apple-tree fairies, also known as the Griggs, the apple tree fairies, so making apple muffins will warm a Griggs fairy's heart.

DIFFICULTY:

TIME: 10 minutes to prepare, 30 minutes to bake

MAKES: 12 muffins

EQUIPMENT: Muffin tray and baking cups

INGREDIENTS:
½ cup melted butter
2 eggs
1 cup milk
2 cups flour
½ cup sugar
1 tablespoon baking powder
½ teaspoon salt

DIRECTIONS: Preheat oven to 400 degrees F. Line a muffin tray with paper baking cups and coat with vegetable oil spray. Set aside.

In a small saucepan melt the butter and set it aside to cool. Whisk together butter, eggs, and milk in a medium mixing bowl.

In a separate bowl, mix together the dry ingredients. Combine the wet and dry ingredients and mix gently, but do not over mix. The batter should be smooth.

Spoon the batter into muffin cups, filling to the top. You can use an ice cream scoop to make the muffins the same size.

Bake at 400 F degrees F for 25 to 30 minutes or until the tops are lightly brown.

MUFFIN COMBINATIONS: Add one or more of the following to the batter:
Blueberries: 1 cup fresh or frozen blueberries
Bananas: Slice 2 bananas or mash up enough to make about 2 cups
Apples: Peel and grate 2 apples and add 1 tablespoon of cinnamon (optional: add ½ cup of raisins if you like them)
Chocolate: 1 cup chocolate chips
Or make up your own!

Morning Glory Muffins

I included these delicious muffins because not only are they healthy and delicious but because of the name. Morning glories are a favorite flower of the fairies, and mornings spent with the fairies are glorious. This is another recipe created by The Baker's Café that first introduced me to carrots in muffins. I love the combination of coconut, apples, and carrots, and I think most fairies would agree.

DIFFICULTY:

TIME: 10 minutes to prepare, 25 minutes to bake

MAKES: 18 muffins

EQUIPMENT: Muffin tray and baking cups

INGREDIENTS:
3 eggs
1 tablespoon buttermilk
1 cup vegetable oil
2 tablespoons vanilla
2 cups flour
1¼ cups sugar
2 teaspoons baking soda
½ teaspoon salt
½ cup raisins (optional)
½ cup coconut (optional)
½ cup chopped walnuts (optional)
1 grated, peeled apple
2 cups fresh grated carrot

DIRECTIONS: Preheat oven to 400 F degrees F. Line a muffin tray with paper baking cups and coat lightly with a vegetable oil spray. Set aside.

In a medium mixing bowl, whisk eggs, then add buttermilk, oil, and vanilla.

In a large bowl, sift together all dry ingredients. Add apples and carrots and gently coat them with the flour mixture. Next, add the wet ingredients to the dry and mix well.

If batter feels too stiff and thick, add more buttermilk, 1 tablespoon at a time, until it is fairly smooth but not too watery.

Spoon the batter into muffin cups, filling to the top. You can use an ice cream scoop to make the muffins the same size.

Bake at 400 degrees F for 25 minutes or until muffins are golden brown.

NOTE: To make your own buttermilk, add a squirt of lemon juice to whole milk. Let rest for 10 minutes before using.

Pancakes

To make pancakes from scratch is as easy as 1, 2, 3, and once you have this recipe down you will be the star of breakfast. Like the muffin recipe, pancakes can have various ingredients and the types of flour used and even the type of milk can be changed. You can even substitute orange juice for milk if you want. I like these with almond milk and white whole-wheat flour. But do not forget to make a tiny one for the fairies every time you and your family have this breakfast treat. It is a small thing, but one that the fairies will greatly appreciate.

DIFFICULTY:
TIME: 20 minutes
MAKES: 6–8 pancakes
EQUIPMENT: Griddle or large frying pan

INGREDIENTS:
2 cups all-purpose flour (or white whole-wheat flour)
1 tablespoon baking powder
½ teaspoon salt
1 or 2 eggs
2 cups milk (or use almond or rice milk or substitute orange juice)
Butter or vegetable oil for cooking

DIRECTIONS: Preheat a griddle or a large frying pan over low heat to warm it up while you prepare the batter.

In a large bowl combine dry ingredients.

In a separate bowl beat the eggs and then add milk. Gently add this to the dry ingredients and stir just enough so everything is combined. Add more milk if the batter seems too thick.

Melt the butter or oil in the frying pan. Use a ladle to pour pancakes into the pan. When bubbles form on the top, flip them. Allow 2 to 4 minutes per side.

If you are adding blueberries: Add 1 cup to batter as the last ingredient added. Chocolate chips can be added directly on top of pancakes as they cook.

OTHER THINGS TO TRY:
Grated apples or sliced pears
Banana slices
Bacon
Crushed and drained pineapple

Perfect Fairy Scones

No fairy tea party or breakfast would be complete without the traditional scone. However, scones are a tricky pastry to perfect. Sometimes they turn out dry and tasteless. Before I tried this recipe, whenever given the choice of a muffin or scone, I would always choose a muffin, but now it is a tough decision. This recipe was adapted from the renowned Savoy Hotel in London. I am sure many fairies have hung around those hallowed halls nibbling on scone crumbles. These are plain scones, but you can add little surprises like currants (which are tiny raisins) or orange zest (which is grated orange peel) and any other bits of fruit you think might be tasty. (Adapted from *friendlyfood.com*)

DIFFICULTY:

TIME: 30 minutes to prepare, 10 minutes to rest dough, 15 minutes to bake.

MAKES: 12 scones

INGREDIENTS:

1¾ cups all-purpose flour

4 teaspoons baking powder (try 1 tablespoon)

¼ cup white sugar

¼ teaspoon salt

5 tablespoons unsalted butter

½ cup milk

¼ cup sour cream or plain yogurt

1 egg

1 tablespoon milk

Optional: currants, orange zest, or other flavors

DIRECTIONS: Preheat the oven to 400 degrees F.

In a large bowl, sift flour, baking powder, sugar, and salt. Add butter and mix between your fingers until it is in pea-size lumps. Stir in any extra addition like currants or orange zest.

Mix together ½ cup milk and sour cream or yogurt in a measuring cup.

Pour all at once into the dry ingredients and stir gently until well blended.

WARNING: Do not mix too much as overworking the dough results in very dry and tough scones!

With floured hands, roll dough into 2- to 3-inch balls, depending on what size you want. Place on a greased baking sheet and flatten lightly.

Whisk together the egg and 1 tablespoon of milk. Brush the tops of the scones with the egg wash. Let them rest for 10 minutes.

Bake for 10 to 15 minutes until the tops are golden brown.

Serve with butter and a selection of different flavored jam.

Magic Puffy Pancakes

(Also known as German Pancakes)

A s I said in the introduction, cooking can be magical, and this recipe is just that. If you've ever had a popover, these puffy, poofy pancakes are a giant version. And anything that is a puffy magic bunch of yumminess will inspire fairy activities.

DIFFICULTY:

TIME: 10 minutes to assemble, 15 to 20 minutes to bake

MAKES: 4–6 servings

EQUIPMENT: 10-inch skillet

INGREDIENTS:

1 tablespoon butter
4 eggs (these are what make the puff puffy)
1 cup milk
1 teaspoon vanilla
3 tablespoons sugar
1 cup all-purpose flour
¼ teaspoon salt

DIRECTIONS: Preheat oven to 450 degrees F. Add tablespoon of butter in 10-inch oven-proof skillet and place in oven.

In large bowl beat eggs with a whisk until frothy and light-colored. Add milk and vanilla and stir. Add sugar, flour, and salt and stir until batter is smooth.

Using a potholder, remove the skillet from the oven or ask a parent to help you, especially if it is heavy. Pour the batter into the pan and return it carefully to the oven.

Bake 15 to 20 minutes and your puff is golden-colored and light brown around the edges. Again, ask a grown-up to help or remove with a pot holder and set to cool for 1 minute. The pancake will begin to deflate but don't worry—that is normal and it will still be delicious!

Cut in wedges and serve right away with your choice of topping: maple syrup, powdered sugar, sliced strawberries, applesauce, or yogurt.

Purple Power Puffs

These magical balls really are purple and they are filled with ingredients that give you power and energy—just like fairy dust! One of my fairy-ish friends, Nicole, who is also one of the best bakers I know, made up this recipe to give her children energy so they can make tons of fairy houses!

DIFFICULTY:

TIME: 15 minutes to assemble, 30 minutes to chill

MAKES: 12 puffs

EQUIPMENT: Food processor

INGREDIENTS:

½ cup oats

½ teaspoon cinnamon

1 cup almonds

1 cup dates

½ cup frozen blueberries (thawed and drained) or fresh

1 tablespoon coconut oil

1 tablespoon maple syrup

DIRECTIONS: Grind oats and cinnamon in food processor then pour into small bowl and set aside.

Grind almonds in food processor, then add dates and remaining ingredients and mix.

Coat your hands with a bit of flour and roll into bite-size balls. Roll them in the oat mixture, place on cookie sheet and chill for 30 minutes.

Gingerbread Dutch Baby

This is the slightly less puffy cousin of Purple Power Puffs and one that is well-suited for fall because of the gingerbread spices. Perhaps you can make this delicious breakfast treat (adapted from the *Smitten Kitchen Cookbook*) on the day you turn your pumpkin into a fall fairy house. I love this recipe because you mix everything in a regular kitchen blender.

DIFFICULTY:

TIME: 10 minutes to prepare, 15 to 20 to bake

MAKES: 2 generous servings or up to 5 smaller ones

EQUIPMENT: Blender

INGREDIENTS:

2 eggs
¼ cup flour
1 tablespoon dark brown sugar
1 teaspoon molasses (maple syrup can be substituted)
¼ teaspoon cinnamon
¼ teaspoon ginger
¼ teaspoon nutmeg
¼ teaspoon salt
¼ cup milk
2 tablespoons unsalted butter

DIRECTIONS: Preheat the oven to 400 degrees F.

Put the eggs in blender and mix until they are frothy and light-colored (about 20 seconds). Add the rest of the ingredients except the butter and blend until combined.

Over medium heat, melt butter in a large oven-proof skillet. Swirl the melted butter up the sides and be sure to cover all sides. Pour the batter into the skillet and place in the oven.

Cook for 15 to 20 minutes, or until the Dutch baby is all puffed up. It might not stay puffed up as it cools but it will still taste yummy.

Dust with powdered sugar before serving.

FOOD INSPIRED
by FAIRIES and FAIRY
HOUSES

ometimes when it is raining or snowing and you can't get outside to build a fairy house, cooking food that is inspired by fairies or fairy houses is the next best thing. Or maybe you just can't get enough of the fairies and want to eat food that resembles things fairies love. The recipes in this section are also good for fairy party days. Or days when a friend who loves fairies is coming over and you want to make a special snack. This section is broken up into four areas of things fairies love: birds and flowers, wands, toadstool mushrooms and fairy houses. As with most of the recipes in this book, make them your own.

WANDS

Abracadabra! One of the first things that comes to mind when thinking of fairies is magic, so what better place to start than with a section on wands, and the bonus is that after you wave these wands and make your magic, then you can have a scrumptious snack.

Pretzel Wands

This is a quick recipe for beginning wand makers. There are a few methods —dipping the pretzels in the white chocolate or brushing it on—but either way you will end up with a snazzy and tasty pretzel wand that is quick to make and even faster to eat.

DIFFICULTY:

TIME: 20 minutes

MAKES: 10 wands

EQUIPMENT: Microwavable bowl (or double boiler if you don't have a microwave), wooden spoon, rubber spatula

INGREDIENTS:
12-ounce bag of white chocolate chips
10 pretzel rods
Waxed paper
Multi-colored decorating sugars and sprinkles or candies

DIRECTIONS: Microwave the white chocolate chips for 15-second intervals until they are nearly melted. Stir the chips until you have a smooth icing. If you don't have a microwave, melt the chocolate chips in a double boiler.

Use a rubber spatula to evenly spread white chocolate on one of the pretzel rods, leaving the bottom inch or so uncoated. Or dip directly into the bowl or saucepan.

Working over a waxed paper-covered surface, generously sprinkle sugar and candies on the white chocolate before it hardens. If it does harden, re-dip or re-spread the chocolate on.

Repeat the process until all pretzels are coated and look fit for magic spells.

Fruit Wands

We know fruit has magical powers, so we know that fairies would love for you to eat a wand filled with rainbow colored fruit. So would your parents! These fruity magic wands will cast a true spell because they will be gone before you know it. There are lots of combinations that you can make here, a favorite is filling the skewer up with blueberries and then cutting a star shape out of a watermelon for the top. Many fruit wand creators use the star fruit as the topper because it is already perfectly formed. But really anything goes in this wand creation and the following is just a list of some possibilities. I leave the ultimate decision to you!

DIFFICULTY:
TIME: 20 minutes
MAKES: 10 wands
EQUIPMENT: Wooden skewers

INGREDIENTS:
Assorted fruit selection: cantaloupe, watermelon, pineapple, blueberries, strawberries, grapes, mango, kiwi, star fruit

DIRECTIONS: You will need wooden skewers (as many as you feel will be enough for family and friends).

Slice the pineapple, star fruit, kiwi, and mango into 1-inch-thick slices. You can use a melon scooper for the watermelon and cantaloupe if you have one.

Slide each fruit onto the skewer in the pattern that you choose. Be careful of the sharp end on the skewer when you are pushing it through the fruit. Voila, your wand is ready to make wishes come true!

Star Cookie Wands

This recipe for shortbread stars is pretty darn yummy without even adding the wand element. So if you are in the mood for a delicious cookie and might not have coffee stirrers or candy sticks on hand, your wish is granted. However, if you have some friends coming over and a free afternoon, decorating star cookie wands makes for a great time. This is not a recipe for those who get easily frustrated. I have had many cookies fall off their stick. But when all goes well, these shortbread cookies will make you feel like you have wings. This recipe is adapted from Ina Garten.

DIFFICULTY:

TIME: 20 minutes to prepare, 30 minutes to chill, 20 to 25 minutes to bake

MAKES: 24 Star Cookies

EQUIPMENT: Star cookie cutter, Kitchenaid mixer or hand-held mixer with paddle attachment, wooden candy sticks

INGREDIENTS:

¾ pound (3 sticks) unsalted butter at room temperature

1 cup sugar

1 teaspoon vanilla extract

3½ cups all-purpose flour

¼ teaspoon salt

DIRECTIONS: Using an electric mixer fitted with a paddle attachment or a hand mixer, in a large bowl mix together the butter and sugar until just combined, then mix in vanilla.

In a medium bowl, mix together flour and salt, then add them to the butter-sugar mixture. Mix on low speed until the dough starts to come together into a big clump.

Dust a counter or cutting board with flour. Roll out the dough and then shape into a flat disk, about 1-inch thick. Wrap in plastic and chill in the refrigerator for 30 minutes, until slightly firm.

Preheat oven to 350 degrees F.

Roll the dough to a ½-inch thickness on a lightly floured surface and cut into star shapes with cookie cutter. Carefully insert candy sticks into star cookies* and arrange on ungreased baking sheet. Sprinkle with sugar.

Bake 20 to 25 minutes or until the edges begin to brown. Remove from oven and allow to cool to room temperature.

*Make sure to mold the shortbread around the stick to really seal it in. When the cookies bake, things expand and shift and sometimes the wands can be wobbly.

So what is it about mushrooms and fairies? Why does every woodland fairy party seem to have a bunch of mushroom crafts and themed food? My guess is that fairies love sitting on mushroom caps. They are soft, yet solid, and provide the perfect spot to survey the forest. And you know about fairy rings, right? A fairy ring is a circle of mushrooms that lets you know the fairies had a party there. They say that if you step in a fairy ring you'll get whisked away to fairyland and it is hard to come back. Another warning, never eat a mushroom you find in the wild or even handle one. They are not good to play around with unless you are an expert in mushrooms.

Toadstool Cupcakes

This is a delicious cupcake made to look like a toadstool. It is not a cupcake made from mushrooms—that would be gross. My friend Hillary, also known as the Camden Cake Lady and mom to expert fairy-house builders Bella and Scarlett, provided this recipe.

DIFFICULTY:

TIME: 10 minutes to prepare, 12 to 15 minutes to bake

MAKES: 12 cupcakes

EQUIPMENT: Cupcake baking pan, cupcake baking papers, electric mixer

INGREDIENTS:

For cupcakes:
1 cup flour
¾ cup sugar
2 teaspoons baking powder
¼ teaspoon salt
¾ stick of butter, softened
½ cup of milk
3 eggs
2 teaspoons vanilla

For the frosting:
2 sticks of butter (softened)
2 cups powdered sugar
2 tablespoons milk
2 teaspoons of vanilla
A few drops of red food coloring
White chocolate chips for the mushroom spots

DIRECTIONS: Preheat oven to 350 degrees F.

Mix the dry ingredients in a mixer bowl of a stand mixer (or use a hand-held mixer and large bowl).

Add butter and mix on medium for one minute. Then add milk, eggs, and vanilla slowly while mixing. Mix for two minutes until batter is smooth.

Place cupcake papers into cupcake pan. Fill cupcake papers with batter to ¾ full.

Bake for 12 to 15 minutes or until golden brown.

Allow to cool before frosting.

To make the frosting:

Mix butter and powdered sugar on medium high for three minutes. Add milk, vanilla, and food coloring, then continue mixing for another four minutes on medium high.

Spread frosting on cupcakes and place the white chocolate chips point side in, on the tops to look like mushroom spots.

Mushroom Meringues

These mushrooms look so much like the real thing that you could set them in a circle on a stump or a fake grass mat to make a "fairy ring." Making meringues allows you to practice your technique for separating egg whites; gently rocking the yolk from one half of the shell to the next to get out all of the excess white takes a lot of practice and concentration. If you want to skip the melted chocolate part of this recipe, no worries. The mushroom stems can be stuck into the caps fairly easily. Use a sifter or a mesh colander to evenly sprinkle the cocoa confection over the mushrooms to give that extra "real dirt" effect. (Adapted from *Allrecipes.com*)

DIFFICULTY:

TIME: 45 minutes to prepare, 60 minutes to bake

EQUIPMENT: Electric mixer and a pastry bag with a round tip

INGREDIENTS:

½ cup egg whites

¼ teaspoon cream of tartar

¼ teaspoon salt

1 teaspoon vanilla extract

1 cup granulated sugar

2 tablespoons powdered sugar

1 teaspoon unsweetened cocoa powder

1 bag chocolate chips

DIRECTIONS: Preheat the oven to 225 degrees F.

In a large glass or metal bowl, use electric mixer to whip egg whites until foamy. Add cream of tartar, salt, and vanilla. Continue whipping until the whites hold soft peaks. Gradually sprinkle in the granulated sugar so that it does not sink to the bottom, and continue whipping until the mixture holds stiff, shiny peaks.

Line two cookie sheets with parchment paper.

Place a round tip into a pastry bag, and fill the bag half way with the meringue. To pipe the mushroom caps, squeeze out round mounds of meringue onto one of the prepared cookie sheets.

Pull the bag off to the side to avoid making peaks on the top. For the stems, press out a tiny bit of meringue onto the second cookie sheet, then pull the bag straight up. They should resemble candy kisses. Do not worry about making all of the pieces exactly the same. The mushrooms will look more natural if the pieces are different sizes.

In a small bowl, mix powdered sugar and cocoa powder. Using a small sifter or strainer, dust the mushroom caps lightly with cocoa powder mixture.

Bake for 1 hour in the preheated oven, or until the caps are dry enough to easily remove from the cookie sheets. Set aside to cool completely.

Melt chocolate chips in a metal bowl over simmering water, or in a glass bowl in the microwave, stirring occasionally until smooth.

Poke a small hole in the bottom of a mushroom cap. Spread chocolate over the bottom of the cap. Dip the tip of a stem in chocolate, and press lightly into the hole. When the chocolate sets, they will hold together. Repeat with remaining pieces.

Store at room temperature in a dry place or tin.

Marzipan Mushrooms

Marzipan is a sweetened almond paste that is kind of like edible clay. People use it to make tiny fruit and other shapes. The only problem is that we like marzipan so much that it sometimes gets eaten before we make the mushrooms! The trick here is finding white colored marzipan. It is okay if you can't, but your mushrooms will look a little more yellowish. (Adapted from *Fairy Cooking*)

DIFFICULTY:
TIME: 30 minutes
MAKES: 8 mushrooms

INGREDIENTS:
9 ounces white marzipan
red food coloring

DIRECTIONS: Divide marzipan into two equals halves. Wrap one half in plastic wrap and place the other in a small bowl.

Add 3 drops of red food coloring to the bowl and mix it in with a spoon or your fingers. (Your hands will turn red!)

Break the red marzipan into 8 equal pieces. Roll each piece into a ball and take your thumb and forefinger and squash them a bit to make a mushroom shape. Press your thumb into the bottom to make a hollow.

Unwrap the other half of white marzipan. Separate one third of the plain marzipan and roll into tiny balls to use for spots on the mushrooms.

Break the remaining marzipan into 8 stem pieces. Roll each

WARNING
This recipe uses nuts—DO NOT give a mushroom to anyone who has a nut allergy.

piece between your fingers and press a red top on it. Press the little balls of marzipan into the red caps of each mushroom.

Store extra mushrooms in an airtight container but make sure to eat them within 3 weeks.

Tiny Food

There are people who specialize in making tiny food for dollhouses, but what about tiny food for fairy houses? Think about all of the ways you could create little food for the fairies. One idea is to coat Cheerios with icing to look like tiny frosted donuts. Or shape marzipan into tiny fruit and paint it with watered down food coloring and brushes. You can watch a YouTube video on how to make marzipan fruit. What other tiny food creations can you think of?

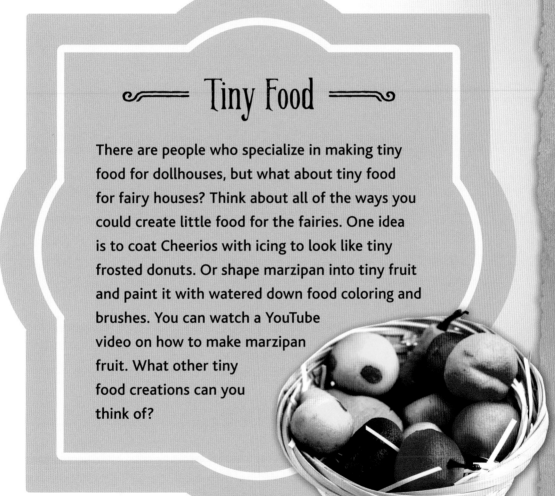

Fairies and birds are very good friends and they say that fairies can even understand birdsong. If you take care of the birds, the fairies will be very happy. The same goes for flowers. There is an entire fleet of flower fairies committed to taking care of them. These recipes will fill the fairies' hearts with gladness and your stomach with sweet delights.

Speedy Garden Patch Cake

When I first discovered this cake recipe that could be assembled in minutes, I had my reservations. I mean how could a cake only take six-minutes to make and still be good? But it was good and made me think this must be a fairy cake because it is one of the easiest and most delicious cakes in my collection. And because of the way the vinegar mixes with the baking soda, there is a lovely swirl that you can watch as you stir. Since the cake is so quick and easy to make, it leaves you lots of time to decorate and create a full garden complete with dirt, worms, raspberries, gummy bugs, and even fake flowers. (Adapted from the "Six-Minute Chocolate Cake" that appeared in *House and Garden* magazine in 1976.)

DIFFICULTY:

TIME: 10 minutes to prepare, 30 minutes to bake, decorating time is really up to you

MAKES: 8 servings

INGREDIENTS:

For cake:
1½ cups unbleached flour
⅓ cup unsweetened cocoa powder
1 teaspoon baking soda
½ teaspoon salt
1 cup sugar
½ cup vegetable oil
1 cup cold water
2 teaspoons vanilla extract
2 tablespoons white vinegar

For frosting:
Chocolate Frosting (store bought to go
   with the speedy theme)
Oreos or Chocolate
Wafers ground up
Gummy worms
Mint leaves
Artificial Flowers

DIRECTIONS: In an ungreased 8-inch square or 9-inch round cake pan combine flour, cocoa, baking soda, salt, and sugar.

In a 2-cup measuring cup (or use a small bowl if you don't have one of these), measure and combine the oil, water, and vanilla. Pour the liquids into the mixture in the pan and mix well with a whisk or a fork.

Add the vinegar and stir quickly. You will see pale swirls from the vinegar and baking soda reacting.

Bake for 25 to 30 minutes. Allow to cool before you frost and decorate.

After frosting, grind the Oreos in a food processor or blender, or crush them in a sealed plastic bag. Spread over the frosting. Then stick the worms and other garden creatures in the dirt. Dig in!

BIRD'S NEST COOKIES

There are two versions of this very delicious and
authentic looking bird's nest cookie, one that uses
nuts and one that doesn't. I would also say that
the first one might have a few more "twigs" in it,
while the second uses "branches."

Nut Free Bird's Nest Cookies

These might be messier bird's nests than your average robin's nest but they are much tastier. Just as birds often add bits and pieces from their flights, you can add more to this recipe such as coconut flakes, raisin bran, or even pretzels.

DIFFICULTY:

TIME: 15 minutes to assemble, 20 minutes to chill

MAKES: 12 servings

EQUIPMENT: kitchen scissors or household scissors that you have scrubbed clean, muffin tin

INGREDIENTS:
1 12-ounce bag milk chocolate chips
1 12-ounce bag butterscotch chips
1 12-ounce bag of chow mein noodles
1 cup of shredded wheat cereal
Chocolate eggs, M&Ms, or jelly beans to fill the nest, if desired

DIRECTIONS: Grease a muffin tin and set aside.

In a large microwave-safe bowl, melt chocolate chips and butterscotch chips together, stirring every 30 seconds. You can also melt the chips in a double boiler.

When the chips are melted and smooth, stir in chow mein noodles and broken-up shredded wheat cereal.

Spoon the nest mixture into the greased muffin tins and mold into the shape of birds' nests. To firm nests more quickly, place them in the refrigerator for about 20 minutes.

Nutty Bird's Nest Cookies

The difference here is instead of butterscotch and chow mein noodles, you add peanut butter and pretzels. These can also be molded into a perfect nest shape to hold candy eggs or even a thin layer of edible fairy dust (see page 94). (Adapted from *twopeasandtheirpod.com*)

DIFFICULTY:

TIME: 15 minutes to assemble, 20 minutes to chill

MAKES: 24 cookies

EQUIPMENT: kitchen scissors or household scissors that you have scrubbed clean

INGREDIENTS:
½ cup unsalted butter
½ cup milk
2 cups granulated sugar
¼ cup unsweetened cocoa
½ cup creamy peanut butter
1 teaspoon vanilla extract
2½ cups old fashioned oats
1 cup chopped pretzels
¼ teaspoon sea salt
NOTE: You can make these gluten free by using gluten free oats and pretzels!

DIRECTIONS: In a medium saucepan, melt butter over medium heat. Add milk, sugar, and cocoa and stir to combine while bringing to a boil.

Boil for 1 to 2 minutes, stirring occasionally. Remove pan from heat. Add in peanut butter and vanilla, and stir until smooth. Stir in oats, chopped pretzels, and sea salt.

Drop mixture by spoonfuls onto waxed paper and mold into the shape of birds' nests. Cookies will harden when they cool.

Store in an airtight container for up to four days.

WARNING Nuts are used so DO NOT make these if anyone close to you has a nut allergy.

Fairy Hearts or Elf Ear Cookies

These delicate, easy, and delicious cookies are based on a traditional French cookie called Palmiers. They are also known as "Elephant Ears." This recipe reduces the ear size so that they actually resemble Elf ears. But if you find the idea of munching on an Elf's ear a little unsettling, then imagine they are enchanted fairy hearts. I prefer these cookies fresh out of the oven, when the pastry is still warm. They will keep for a few days, if they aren't all eaten in one sitting.

DIFFICULTY:

TIME: 15 minutes to prepare and 15 minutes to bake

MAKES: 15–20 cookies

INGREDIENTS:

⅛ teaspoon salt

½ cup sugar

1 sheet Pepperidge Farm puff pastry, defrosted

DIRECTIONS: Preheat oven to 450 degrees F.

Mix the salt into the sugar and pour over half of it on a flat surface such as a large cutting board. Spread the sugar evenly over the surface and then unfold the defrosted puff pastry and place on top of the sugar. Pour the remaining sugar over the pastry. Using a rolling pin, gently roll the sugar so that it presses into the dough.

Fold each side of the square sheet into the center so they meet halfway in the middle. Then, fold them again so the two folds are in the middle again. Then, like you are closing a book, fold one half of the dough over the other half which will result in a six-layer dough.

Slice the dough into thin ½-inch slices and place on a parchment lined baking sheet. Arrange them cut side up.

Bake for 6 minutes until the bottoms are caramelized and brown. Have a grown-up pull out the baking sheet from the oven and flip over because the sugar is very hot and can burn easily. Cook the other side for 3 to 5 minutes and then remove from the oven.

If you have spent endless hours building fairy houses, then you know that the main rule is to be creative. All of the following recipes follow that same rule. The idea is to use things like ice cream cones, watermelons, and graham crackers instead of bark and sticks. But there is even a recipe for bark—the chocolate kind. The difference is that you can eat these after the fairies come to visit. A nice bonus!

Chocolate Bark

Since bark is an essential component in creating a true fairy house, I thought it would be good to include the kind of bark you can eat. If you would like to make a chocolate bark fairy house, go ahead. Take four pieces of the bark and lean them up against each other to make a square. Then create a roof with orange peels and lettuce leaves. Create a pathway with blueberries and pomegranate seeds and the fairies will be sure to come for a snack! According to chocolate-bark expert Abby Michalski, "You don't need a recipe, or even to measure any ingredients, to make gorgeous chocolate bark—it's about getting creative and using your favorite flavors and textures."

You can use whatever chocolate you have on hand and top your bark with things like nuts and seeds for added crunch. Pistachios add a nice splash of color, as do dried fruits, such as raisins, currants, cherries, chopped dates, figs, apricots, or finely sliced mango.

DIFFICULTY:
TIME: 3 hours
MAKES: 24 cookies
EQUIPMENT: Double boiler, baking sheet, baker's parchment paper

INGREDIENTS:
24 ounces milk chocolate

DIRECTIONS: Bring water to a boil over high heat in the bottom of a double boiler. Once boiling reduce heat to medium high. Break your chocolate into the top part of the double boiler. Stir with a spoon or spatula until smooth and completely melted.

Line a baking sheet with parchment paper. Pour the melted chocolate onto the lined tray and spread evenly using a spatula. You can make it as thin as you like.

While the chocolate is still soft, add your toppings. Be creative!

Transfer to the fridge for a couple of hours to cool. When completely set, break up into rough shards. Store in an airtight container for a quick sweet treat.

Stained Glass Fairy Door & Window Cookies

This type of cookie is often made around the holidays and is sometimes not even eaten but used for decorating the tree or for hanging in windows. Instead of the traditional star shape, you can create amazing fairy door and fairy house windows. Use the dough as your "wood trim" and fill the windows with stained glass. Maybe a fairy will be tempted to come right through that door to gobble up your cookie! (Adapted from Emeril Lagasse's Stained Glass Star Cookie recipe)

DIFFICULTY:

TIME: 90 minutes to prepare, 10 to 15 minutes to bake

MAKES: 24 cookies

EQUIPMENT: Electric mixer with paddle attachment

INGREDIENTS:

1 cup sugar
2 sticks butter
2 eggs
1 teaspoon pure vanilla extract
3 cups all-purpose flour
Assorted brightly colored, hard candies like Jolly Ranchers or lifesavers

DIRECTIONS: Preheat oven to 350 degrees F.

In a mixer with a paddle attachment, cream the sugar and butter until smooth. Add the egg and vanilla. Mix in the flour slowly. Remove the dough from the mixer and press into a rectangular shape. Wrap in plastic wrap and refrigerate for at least 1 hour.

Remove from the refrigerator and cut dough into thirds. Roll out dough, 1 piece at a time to a half-inch thickness. Using a dull knife, cut squares or rectangles out of the dough. Then carefully cut out smaller squares inside these squares to make a frame.

Place the hard candy, by color, into small plastic ziploc bags. Place a towel over the bags and crush the candy with a rolling pin. Place all of the cookies on parchment lined sheet pans. Fill each of the windows with different colors of crushed hard candy. Bake in the oven for 10 to 15 minutes or until the cookies are golden brown and the candy has melted.

You can eat and enjoy the cookies or use them as windows and doors on fairy houses, such as the Graham Cracker Fairy Cottage (p. 56).

Graham Cracker Fairy Cottage

My apologies to the Gingerbread Man, but it is high time fairies get to enjoy munching on a cookie house too. Basically, these are similar to the graham cracker gingerbread houses that you have most likely made for years. The difference is that now you are thinking not of Christmas but of fairy houses. As you decorate, no need to add snow, opt instead for green icing to represent grass and chocolate pebbles and seashells to line the pathways.

DIFFICULTY: 🦋

TIME: About an hour

MAKES: 1 house

EQUIPMENT: Cardboard for the base, aluminum foil, pastry bag (or a ziploc bag with the corner cut off), electric mixer

INGREDIENTS:

For the frosting:
3 egg whites
½ teaspoon cream of tartar
1 teaspoon vanilla
1 box confectioners' sugar
(You can also buy store bought frosting if you would like.)

For the Houses:
1 box of graham crackers
Decorations: Coconut, jelly beans, gummy bears, animal crackers, life savers, gummy raspberries, etc.

DIRECTIONS: Prepare your base by covering cardboard with aluminum foil.

To make the frosting: In a medium bowl, whip egg whites with an electric mixer until they are fluffy and have stiff peaks. Add cream of tartar and then vanilla. Stir in the confectioner's sugar a little at a time so you don't get a sugar cloud poof.

Spoon the frosting (fairy house glue) into a pastry bag or ziploc bag with the bottom corner cut off. Spread the remaining frosting onto the cardboard so the graham crackers can stick into the icing.

Place graham crackers into the frosting to make four walls. Use frosting in the pastry bag to seal the edges of the walls together. Add two graham crackers for a roof.

Use the frosting to adhere the decorations to your fairy cottage.

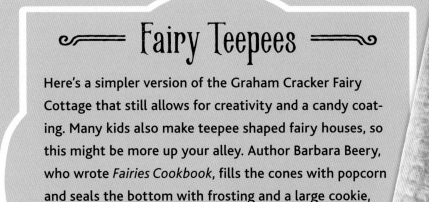

Fairy Teepees

Here's a simpler version of the Graham Cracker Fairy Cottage that still allows for creativity and a candy coating. Many kids also make teepee shaped fairy houses, so this might be more up your alley. Author Barbara Beery, who wrote *Fairies Cookbook*, fills the cones with popcorn and seals the bottom with frosting and a large cookie, which adds a sweet surprise.

Use the same frosting recipe, but substitute sugar ice-cream cones for the graham crackers. Simply stand the cones on the frosting-covered cardboard, coat them with frosting, and add your candy coating in whatever way you think will please the fairies!

Watermelon Fairy House

Watermelons make a perfect domed fairy cottage. You will definitely need an adult to cut this out for you as watermelon rind is tough to get through, but the shape that emerges is sure to enchant the summer fairies.

DIRECTIONS: Have an adult cut a large watermelon in half. Using a melon scoop or spoon, carve out the delicious fruit—you can use this to make Fruit Wands (p. 35). Using a permanent marker, draw windows and a door so your adult knows where to cut. Once these features are cut out, you can decorate the watermelon using different colored permanent markers as well as gluing on things like shutters, a chimney, and roof tiles. Although this fairy house will not stay around forever, it is a fun summery tribute to the fairies.

Pumpkin Fairy House

Very similar to the watermelon fairy house, the pumpkin fairy house requires sharp knives and an adult's help. Instead of carving a jack-o-lantern face, you are carving the front of a house with windows and doors. Or you can just cut out an entire circle, hollow out the pumpkin and use it as a place for your fairy furnishings.

DIRECTIONS: The first step is to cut off the top of the pumpkin and scoop out the gooey insides. (Be sure to save the seeds to roast for a snack and to leave out for the fairies and birds.) Then, as you did for the watermelon house, outline the areas you want cut with a permanent marker. Ask an adult to cut out the windows and doors and then you can add twig ladders for the fairies to climb into their giant pumpkin.

To make a twig ladder, find two thin sticks that are equal in length. Then break up another stick into two-inch lengths. Glue each end of the smaller twigs onto the longer sticks to make a ladder.

FAIRY FORAGING

Imagine you are a fairy, flitting about from flower to flower, fairy house to fairy house, occasionally munching on a berry or sipping a bit of nectar from a honeysuckle. When we gather our food from nature, we are following in the path of fairies. That is what foraging means, to collect food from its source, whether from a bush, a tree, or a field. It also means, "the act of searching for provisions of any kind." There are so many delicious things to gather, such as raspberries, strawberries, blueberries, pears, apples, edible flowers, and more.

Sitting and eating berry after berry is grand, but you can flex your baking muscles by creating some delicious desserts with your recently foraged finds. Just like in the breakfast section, where we discussed how you can add different ingredients to the muffin recipe or pancakes, this section has a mix-and-match quality too. The pie crust can be used for apples or strawberries. Any kind of fruit can be used in the quick tart and cobbler. Once you have finished your freshly foraged dessert, you can decorate it with Candied Violets or other edible flowers. One trick a fairy friend told me to guarantee a good harvest, is to always thank the fairies as you gather flowers or fruit. Be gentle as you pick nature's candy and remember to only take what you need.

WARNING
This section talks mainly about things like apples from the orchard and raspberries from the patch, not wild mushrooms or unknown berries. Never pick a mushroom or a berry and put it in your mouth until a grown up with very good knowledge of wild food has identified it.
Seriously.

Candied Violets

"It is believed that fairies were at one time responsible for drawing the faces on Johnny Jump-ups, and upon close inspection, the center of the flower reveals a 'bewhiskered kitty face.'"

— Dawn Hylton Gottlieb and Diane Sedo

One of the earliest spring flowers is the violet. Fairies have a special relationship to this flower as it is a favorite of the fairy queen and used in almost all of the spring celebrations. This recipe (Adapted from *Taste of Home*) works only if you use the wild purple violets and not the houseplant called African violet. This process can be a little tricky so get your extra set of patience out of the closet.

DIFFICULTY:

TIME: 20 minutes to prepare, 30 minutes to bake or allow to sit overnight

EQUIPMENT: A small paint brush and a pastry bag with a plain tip

INGREDIENTS:
2 egg whites
2 tablespoons water
At least 1 cup of sugar
1 large bunch wild violets (including stems), washed

DIRECTIONS: Preheat oven to 200 degrees F.

In a medium bowl, beat egg whites with a wire whisk until they become frothy. Add water. Pour sugar into another bowl.

Pick up one violet by the stem and gently paint it with egg white mixture, making sure to cover all surfaces. Gently dip the violet into the sugar, making sure all the petals are completely covered. Place on waxed paper-lined baking sheets, then snip off stems.

Using a toothpick, open petals to original shape. Sprinkle sugar on any uncoated areas. Dry in a 200-degree F oven for 30 to 40 minutes or until sugar crystallizes. If your oven is too hot, the flowers will turn brown and the sugar will get syrupy. An alternative is to let the flowers sit overnight to harden on their own.

Gently remove violets to wire racks with a spatula or two-tined fork. Sprinkle again with sugar if violets appear syrupy. Let cool.

Store in airtight containers with waxed paper between layers.

Edible Flowers

Have you ever smelled a certain flower and wondered if it tasted as good as it smelled? Well, some do. Roses, for example, taste almost exactly the way they smell. But, eating flowers, really?

"Humans all over the world have a long history of eating flowers," says Charlie Nardozzi, edible flower expert. The flowers from cooking herbs, such as thyme, rosemary, and basil, are always edible, as are the flowers on many vegetables, such as peas and radishes. **BUT—and this is very important— not all flowers are edible. In fact, sampling some flowers can make you very sick. And never eat flowers that have been treated with a pesticide or harvest flowers growing by the roadside.** Below is a list of some of the most common edible flowers—you might even have some of them growing in your garden. The best time to gather flowers is in the morning. Soak them in a bowl of water to make sure no bugs hitched a ride, then eat or cook them immediately. Fresh flowers won't keep for too long once picked, so "gather ye rosebuds while ye may!"

BORAGE: These purple star-shaped flowers taste a little bit like cucumbers. They make a nice addition to salads and are good in lemonade.

CHIVE: These flowers taste a lot like their stems, oniony, so they aren't great to top cupcakes. Stick them in your egg salad or in a soup and they will add a nice flavor.

NASTURTIUM: With its bright orange, yellow, and red flowers, these have a real peppery zing. They are so lovely that many people use them to decorate plates (called garnish) and top salads.

PANSY AND VIOLET: It is hard to describe the flavor of these flowers because they are a mix of peppery and minty, but with a little candy coating, they are extra sweet.

ROSE: These somehow taste just the way they smell, so it feels as if you are eating perfume. But when sprinkled over ice cream or as a topping to a cupcake, it is the perfect flavor booster.

HONEYSUCKLE: Nothing says summer like sucking the sweet nectar from a honeysuckle. Pick off the bottom of the flower and drink the nectar. Rrepeat. Yum!

OTHER EDIBLE FLOWERS: Basil flowers, bachelor's buttons, calendula, dahlia, garlic flowers, lavender, marigold, orchids, snapdragons, apple blossom, dianthus.

The Best Pie Crust

I have been making this pie crust since I was a little girl helping my mom make Thanksgiving pies. I have always loved watching as the ingredients magically form into a ball in the food processor. Many people think making pie crusts is tricky and takes forever, but this one literally takes five minutes.

DIFFICULTY:

TIME: 5 to 10 minutes to prepare, 1 hour to set

MAKES: 2 pie crusts

EQUIPMENT: Food processor

INGREDIENTS:

2½ cups all-purpose flour

1 teaspoon salt

1 teaspoon sugar

2 sticks unsalted butter, chilled and cut into small pieces

¼ to ½ cup ice water

DIRECTIONS: In the bowl of a food processor, combine flour, salt, and sugar. Add butter, and pulse for about 10 seconds until the mixture resembles corn meal.

With the food processor running, add half of the ice water through feed tube. Pulse until dough holds together and turns into a ball. Make sure it isn't too wet. Do not process for more than 30 seconds as this will lead to really tough pie crust. To test, take a small amount and squeeze it: If it is crumbly, add more ice water, 1 tablespoon at a time.

Divide dough into two equal balls and flatten into a disc. Wrap each one in plastic and put them in the refrigerator for at least 1 hour. Dough can be stored in the freezer for up to 1 month.

Wild Blueberry Pie

I n Maine where I live, you can gather wild blueberries as you hike. We have often come home from a favorite hike with bags of tiny blueberries to create delicious blueberry treats. But there is nothing that says summer like a traditional blueberry pie. This recipe is from Lynda Chilton, the amazingly talented designer who has designed all of my books. Turns out she is also a very talented baker!

DIFFICULTY:

TIME: 15 minutes to assemble, 40 to 50 minutes to bake

MAKES: 1 pie

INGREDIENTS:

5½ cups of wild blueberries (washed and stemmed)
4 tablespoons flour
½ cup sugar
1 teaspoon of fresh lemon juice
pinch of salt
¼ teaspoon cinnamon
2 pie crusts
1 beaten egg
Sugar in the raw for sprinkling on the top of the crust

DIRECTIONS: Preheat oven to 400 degrees F.

Pour blueberries into a large bowl. Gently stir flour, sugar, lemon juice, salt, and cinnamon into the blueberries.

Press first pie crust into a 9-inch glass pie pan. Pour blueberry mixture onto the crust and spread evenly.

Cover berries with second crust and pinch the edges together. Make 3 slashes in the center of the top crust to vent. With a pastry brush, spread the beaten egg over the pie. Sprinkle with a fine dusting of raw sugar. This makes a more lushly browned and sparkly pie!

Place pie pan on cookie sheet to catch any juice overflow.

Bake for 40 to 50 minutes or until crust is golden brown.

Allow to cool.

Apple Cobbler

Having a good fruit cobbler recipe in your back pocket means you always have something quick and delicious to do with fresh fruit. This recipe uses apples, which are plentiful in the fall. There is nothing like coming home from a day of picking apples, preparing a cobbler, and then smelling it in the oven as it bakes. This recipe comes from Hope Orchard, our favorite local orchard in the tiny town of Hope, Maine, and was created by Emily, one of the owners of the orchard.

DIFFICULTY: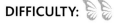

TIME: 30 minutes to prepare and 35 minutes to bake

EQUIPMENT: 9x13-inch baking dish

INGREDIENTS:

6–8 peeled and cored apples
¾ cup sugar
¼ cup flour
1 teaspoon cinnamon

For topping:
1 cup flour
1 cup oats
1 cup brown sugar
½ cup melted butter

DIRECTIONS: Preheat oven to 375 degrees F.

Butter a 9x13-inch baking dish. Peel and core the apples and combine them with sugar, flour, and cinnamon. Toss together until well mixed and then put them in the baking dish. In a small bowl mix the flour, oats, and brown sugar with the melted butter. Press this onto the apples to form a topping. Bake for 35 minutes or until apples or just barely soft.

Mini Plum Tartlets

This recipe is a quick one and allows you to make a variety of different mini pies, also known as tartlets. If you are wanting a quick treat, use store-bought crust or follow the previous pie crust recipe. Also, you can substitute other fruit such as nectarines, peaches, or apple.

DIFFICULTY:

TIME: 15 minutes to assemble, 20 minutes to bake

MAKES: 4 tartlets

INGREDIENTS:
1 pie crust
¼ cup fig jam
2 plums
1 tablespoon brown sugar
2 tablespoons melted butter

DIRECTIONS: Preheat oven to 375 degrees F.

NOTE: this recipe requires only one pie crust, half of The Best Pie Crust (p. 66); or you can use both crusts and double the recipe to make 8 tartlets.

Roll crust out onto a lightly floured surface. Using a jar lid or a small glass, stamp out four four-inch round circles in the pie crust. Spread fig jam inside the circles, leaving a half-inch edge all around.

Slice plums thinly and lay slices in the center of the circles. Use about half of a plum per circle. Then gather and pull up the edges of the crust around the fruit like you are tucking them in.

Top fruit slices with a sprinkle of brown sugar. Brush the crusts and plums with melted butter.

Bake at 375 degrees F for 20 minutes, or until the crusts are golden.

4
FAIRY PARTIES

"It's a very special honor to be invited
to tea with the fairies, for only those
who truly believe will be blessed with
the rewards of their presence."

~Dawn

airies and tea parties go hand in hand. What better way to celebrate your love of fairies, and your new found love of cooking fairy food than to have a fairy tea party. There is nothing better on a beautiful summer day than to gather your friends together to sip tea, talk about fairy sightings, and eat delicious food.

But fairy parties can happen anytime throughout the year, inside or out. Anytime you have a feeling that you need to pay tribute to your fairy friends, then a party is in order. This section will prepare you to make your fairy party the best it can be. There are tips to make a perfect pot of tea and recipes to make your party the hit of fairy season.

Setting the Scene

You can enhance the scenery for your tea party by sewing a garland of blossoms threaded with a needle and string to festoon around the party area. A giant daisy or dandelion chain would also be festive. Place a table covered in a prettytablecloth in the center of your party and set it with a vase of fresh-picked flowers as well as your tea set. If you have a good idea who is coming, make some place cards so friends will know where they are sitting. If you have a tiny chair from a dollhouse or play mobile, set that out and maybe a fairy will join you at the gathering!

Generally, when people come over, it is polite to offer them something to drink. Here are several festive and thirst-quenching recipes so you don't have to just offer water.

Healthy Bubbly

There are lots of ways to not only make a healthy version of soda but to make it your own. The beauty of homemade soda is that you control the flavor and the amount of bubbles.

DIFFICULTY:

TIME: 10 minutes

MAKES: 4 4-oz drinks

EQUIPMENT: large measuring cup

INGREDIENTS

8 tablespoons of frozen juice concentrate: your choice of lemonade, orange juice, cranberry, apple, or all mixed together

2 cups sparkling water

DIRECTIONS: In a large measuring cup, stir and mash the frozen concentrate until it gets soft.

Add sparkling water and stir.

Add fairy-licious ice cubes and enjoy.

Honey Lemon Fizz

Although similar to the healthy soda above, this drink uses honey as a sweetener and lemon. Fairies love honey—they are good friends with the bees after all—so leave an acorn cap full of this delicious drink to quench their thirst after a long day of tending to the garden.

DIFFICULTY: 🦋
TIME: 10 minutes
MAKES: 6 6-oz drinks
EQUIPMENT: Small pitcher

INGREDIENTS:
3 cups sparkling water
3 to 5 teaspoons honey (depending
  on preference)
Lemon juice

DIRECTIONS: In a small pitcher, combine sparkling water, honey, and two squirts of lemon juice. Stir well so the honey is absorbed in the mixture. Pour into individual cups.

Icy Berry Slushy

No need to go to the Dairy Queen, this special homemade version of a slushy has a fraction of the sugar and a thousand times more real, fresh fruit. A great treat for a hot summer day.

DIFFICULTY:

TIME: 10 minutes

MAKES: 3 6-oz servings or
2 8-oz servings

EQUIPMENT: Blender

INGREDIENTS:
20 to 25 strawberries
4 teaspoons lemon juice
1 tablespoon sugar
10 or 12 ice cubes

DIRECTIONS: Blend all the ingredients until slushy and smooth. If it seems too thick, add a little water. Pour into cups and slurp away.

How to Make a
~ Proper Pot of Tea ~

The most important thing about making a cup of tea is to have really hot water—As hot as you can get it! And you must have a very good teapot. The best kind of teapots are round and made of red clay. English fairies call these teapots "Brown Betty's." The red clay is very good at keeping the tea warm and the round shape of the teapot helps the tea leaves circulate.

First, take a small amount of the very hot water and put it in the teapot to "warm" it. After a few minutes, dump the water out. Add 2 to 3 teaspoons of your favorite tea and fill the teapot with the hot water. Smell the fragrance! Place the lid on the pot and let it brew for 3 to 5 minutes. You can help it along by giving the teapot a little swirl. If it's cold weather you can put a tea cozy on the pot to keep it warm. (A tea cozy is like a knitted sweater in bright colors.) Warmth is what makes the tea leaves give up all their flavor!

Next, place a tea strainer (to catch the tea leaves) over your cup and pour the tea. Most English fairies like milk and lumps of sugar in their tea. Pink sugar lumps are especially fancy! Most put their milk in first and then pour the hot tea and add sugar to taste. But as long as your tea is well-brewed it doesn't really matter. Some fairies like lemon in their tea and sweeten it with honey. But nearly all of them like a second cup of tea, regardless!

—Hazel Mitchell, illustrator of *Where Do Fairies Go When It Snows?*
and *Do Fairies Bring the Spring?*

Fairy Cakes

Many people have fond memories of making fairy cakes with their grandparents. These spongy and delicious mini cakes are perfect for a summer tea party. The best part is decorating them with a sweet glaze and sprinkles, dried flower petals, or tiny candies.

(Adapted from *Betty Bib's Fairy Handbook*)

DIFFICULTY:

TIME: 1 hour

MAKES: 12–18 cakes

Equipment: Muffin baking pan and paper muffin cases

INGREDIENTS:

For the cakes:
4 ounces butter, softened
4 ounces sugar
2 medium eggs, beaten
1 teaspoon vanilla
4 ounces self-rising flour
2 tablespoons milk

For the icing:
4 ounces powdered sugar
Juice of 1 lemon
Flavorings: Vanilla, lemon or orange zest, almond essence, rose essence

Toppings: Colored crystal sugar, lavender flowers, sprinkles, candies

DIRECTIONS: Preheat oven to 375 degrees F. Have ready 12 to 18 paper muffin cases. These cakes SHOULD be small and dainty, NOT standard "muffin" size. Cream butter or margarine with sugar until light, fluffy, and pale in color. Beat the eggs and vanilla and add them bit by bit to the butter/sugar mixture with spoons of sifted flour. Then stir in the milk. Add choice of flavoring to taste.

Half fill the paper cases with the mixture and bake for 15 minutes or until risen and firm and golden brown. Cool them on a wire rack.

To make the icing, put the powdered sugar in a bowl and add the lemon juice. Beat together until the icing is thick enough to stick on the back of a spoon.

Decorate with some of the suggested toppings, dust with extra icing sugar, and watch them fly away!

You are Invited!

Invitations

Planning a party can be elaborate or spur of the moment. Once you have an idea of when to have your party, make a list of friends to invite. Maybe you have friends who feel the same way about fairies as you do and will truly appreciate your hard work, or maybe you have some who just love eating cookies. No matter, make your list and get ready to create some invitations. An invitation can be as fancy or simple as you like. One idea is to cut paper into a tea-cup shape and write the invitation on that. Include a real tea bag of your favorite kind of tea for your friends to enjoy. You can also write your invitation on a hosta leaf in a gold pen and hand deliver the message. However you decide to create the invitation, make sure to put the time, date, rain date, location, and a phone number so people can let you know if they are coming.

Real Fairy Bread

airy bread is a traditional Australian childhood favorite that appears at almost all kids' birthday parties, but it can also be made for fairy parties, May Day, or the Summer Solstice. A fairy cookbook would not be complete without this recipe and you would not be a fairy cook if you didn't have this one in your repertoire.

DIFFICULTY:
TIME: 5 minutes
MAKES: as much or as little as you need for your party

INGREDIENTS:
White bread
Softened butter or margarine
Bright colored sprinkles

DIRECTIONS: Simply spread the butter on the bread and sprinkle with a selection of rainbow colored sprinkles. Cut in triangles and serve.

Healthy Fairy Bread

True fairy enthusiasts might be horrified that I am offering a healthy, protein-rich version of fairy bread with only a touch of sweetness. But it's really all about the magic of decorating the bread and I promise you won't even miss the white bread or the butter.

DIFFICULTY:

TIME: 5 minutes

MAKES: 4–6 servings

INGREDIENTS:
½ teaspoon cinnamon
2 tablespoons sugar
Whipped cream cheese
Soft whole wheat bread with
    crusts cut off
Dried coconut
½ cup of blueberries (the smaller
the better)

DIRECTIONS: Mix the cinnamon and sugar together.

As with Real Fairy Bread, simply spread the cream cheese on the bread with a butter knife, then sprinkle with the cinnamon sugar. Next sprinkle on coconut and add the blueberries. Cut into triangles and serve.

Fairy Trifle

his trifle is an easy but dramatic way to dress up a fairy party. And the beauty of a trifle is that there is no one way to do it. You can either make the cake using the Toadstool Cupcake recipe (p. 38), or buy a pre-made angel food cake or pound cake. This recipe comes from the Camden Cake Lady, whose daughter Scarlett is lucky enough to not only have a baker for a mother but she often gets treasures from the fairies.

DIFFICULTY:

TIME: 10 to 15 minutes (if all ingredients are pre-made, including the pudding)

MAKES: 6–10 servings

INGREDIENTS

White cake, pound cake, or
 angel food cake
Vanilla pudding (follow instructions
 on box or buy ready-made)
Whipped cream
Any combination of fruit (especially
 bananas, raspberries, blueberries,
 blackberries, or strawberries)
Caramel, raspberry, or chocolate sauce
Nuts, sprinkles, mint leaves, cherry
 on top, anything goes!

DIRECTIONS: Cut the cake into thin slices.

Make 1 layer of slices in large glass bowl or individual glass cups. Next coat the cake with pudding, then pile fruit on top of the pudding. Add another layer of cake and repeat. Repeat the layers until you reach the top of your glass bowl.

Cover the top with lots of whipped cream and add a cherry on top.

Tea Sandwiches

A tea party would not be complete without some variety of tea sandwiches. Pull out your cookie cutters and a couple of loaves of bread. Cut out pairs of stars, hearts, flowers, then fill each pair of bread with some delicious sandwich fixing. I like cucumber and cream cheese. The most traditional tea sandwich is a watercress sandwich with butter but your friends might like a simple peanut butter and jelly. If you make these ahead of time, cover them with a wet paper towel and saran wrap. They dry out very quickly.

Becca Hunter (*all-about-afternoon-tea.com*) is a true tea party professional. Here are some practical tips to help you make the most of your tea party sandwiches.

 Finger sandwiches should be small. They should only take 2 or 3 bites to eat. It should be possible to pick up the sandwich in one hand. Afternoon tea is a delicate affair and it's hard to be dainty while munching on a large sandwich that you have to hold in both hands.

Fingers, triangles, or squares are all popular shapes, but I prefer triangles. You can see the filling so much better with triangles and it's easier to lay them out in an attractive way.

The crusts should be removed. It's best to remove the crusts after filling the sandwiches so they look better.

Always buy thin or medium sliced bread—never thick— for afternoon tea.

 Serve 3 to 5 different types of sandwich.

Pinwheel Sandwiches

airies love a good circle—think fairy ring—so these "sandwiches" are a great bet for a fairy party. It's fun to fill the tortillas with a variety of colorful food and see what happens when they are sliced into rolls. Be forewarned, cutting these can be messy and you might need to enlist the help of a grown-up.

DIFFICULTY:
TIME: 15 minutes
MAKES: 12–24 servings

INGREDIENTS:
½ cup cream cheese (softened)
2 to 4 6-inch flour tortillas (depending on the size of your party, you can always do more or less)
A few basil leaves, finely chopped
5 chives, finely chopped
Sprig of dill, finely chopped
Salami, ham, or turkey
Avocado, sliced
Tomato, sliced
Lettuce

DIRECTIONS: Spread cream cheese on the tortillas and then sprinkle chopped herbs over the cream cheese.

Combine any or all of the above ingredients in a flat and even layer. Roll carefully —use a little cream cheese to make sure it stays tight.

Slice roll into pinwheels that are about an inch wide.

Pixie Dust Popcorn

This is a simple way to turn plain old popcorn into a pixie prize. It is always nice to have a crunchy snack option at a party, especially one coated in white chocolate and sprinkles.

DIFFICULTY:
TIME: 25 minutes
MAKES: 10–12 servings

INGREDIENTS:
1 cup popcorn kernels
2 tablespoons vegetable oil
½ cup white chocolate chips
Rainbow colored sprinkles

DIRECTIONS: In a big stockpot, heat up the oil on medium-high heat. Put two popcorn kernels in while the oil heats. When the kernels pop, add the rest of the kernels. Have an adult shake the pan while the popcorn pops so it doesn't get burned. Do not open the lid as steam will escape and can burn you.

Once the popcorn has cooled down, pour it into a large mixing bowl. Melt white chocolate in a microwave- safe bowl or a double-boiler. Pour over the popcorn and quickly coat it with the rainbow sprinkles. Use wooden salad forks to mix it all around so as many kernels get covered as possible.

Flower Fairy Popsicles

opsicles are the epitome of summer, but you don't always need to buy them at the store because they are so easy to make. For a fairy party, just add edible flowers to your frozen pop to make your popsicle really pop.

DIFFICULTY:

TIME: 3 to 4 hours

MAKES: 10–12 servings

EQUIPMENT: Popsicle sticks, a popsicle mold, or Dixie cups

INGREDIENTS:

Edible flowers, such as calendula, marigold, nasturtium, or pansies

Any kind of fruit juice, but lemonade is always a good choice

DIRECTIONS: Fill a Dixie cup or a popsicle mold about three quarters full. Place the popsicles in the freezer. After about ten minutes, pull out your popsicles and place a stick in the center of each popsicle. This step ensures that your popsicle sticks will remain upright. Return them to the freezer.

When the popsicles are frozen through, remove from the freezer. If you used Dixie cups, tear them off. Otherwise gently pull out of the mold. You might need to quickly run the mold under lukewarm water for a few seconds to loosen it from the mold.

If you decide you want to really go crazy making multiple flavors, there is a wonderful book called *Ice Pop Joy* by Anni Daulter that is filled with creative and beautiful frozen treat recipes.

RECIPES *for the* FAIRIES & FRIENDS

airies have a different appetite than we do. They aren't necessarily as hungry in a day as you or I am. They generally enjoy a sip of honey, a little milk, some nectar from a flower, and maybe a little crumble from a baked good. So this section focuses on some recipes that you don't eat, such as fairy dust and birdseed cookies. You'll find recipes to make fairies happy, and the birds and animals happy.

There is also a section of recipes that use natural materials to make backyard stews and soups and yes, my favorite, mud pies. Because I believe that when you make these elaborate backyard concoctions, the fairies are watching as you have fun outside and nothing makes a fairy happier than seeing children enjoying the wonders of nature. So go ahead, mix things up, get muddy and remember to see the world as one big cooking pot.

FAIRY DUST

Making your own fairy dust is not hard and below I offer you three different types, edible, environmentally friendly and wild. But once you've made it, how do you make it magic? Can fairy dust really make you fly? I do not believe that homemade fairy dust can give you flying capabilities (and please do not try to fly from anything higher than a step or two), but I think having a little homemade fairy dust on hand can give you a feeling of magic. And you never know if it will work when you really need it to. My secret for injecting a bit of extra something is to leave the fairy dust outside on a dry night under a full moon.

Edible Fairy Dust

When I say edible here, I don't mean it's okay to eat big bowls of this sugary concoction. But it is biodegradable which means it will dissolve into the earth so it is a good choice when you might be at a botanical garden where glitter is not welcome. You can also sprinkle this on some of the desserts in the previous sections to add even more magic.

INGREDIENTS:
food coloring gel in three different colors
½ cup sugar in the raw divided into three different bowls
3 pieces of 1-foot-long aluminum foil

DIRECTIONS: Preheat oven to 350 degrees F.

Add drops of food coloring into sugar and mix well. Repeat for each different color. Fold up the four sides of the tin foil so it is almost like a little boat. Pour each colored "dust" into each individual tin foil so they don't get mixed up. Bake for 10 minutes so the food coloring bakes into the sugar. Allow pixie dust to cool. Break up the sugar again as it will have melted together a bit. Then store in small fairy-ish containers.

Organic Good-for-the-Earth Fairy Dust

I f you are lucky enough to have mica in your backyard or neighborhood, then this recipe can become a real staple. Otherwise, you can find mica online or if you travel to mountainous areas. Basically, mica crumbles very easily and forms a very shiny, glittery powder. Mix 1 cup of playground sand or cornstarch with at least 2 tablespoons of mica. Add more mica to increase the shine.

INGREDIENTS:
1 cup sand or cornstarch
2 tablespoons ground up mica

Swirly Sparkly Fairy Dust

INGREDIENTS:
Ground up colored chalk
Various colored glitter

Glittery Fairy Face Paint

his is a great recipe to have on hand when you want to feel what may be called fairy-ish. And because it has cold cream as an ingredient, it is actually good for your skin. The trick is not to get it near your eyes or mouth. You can fill empty baby food containers with this paint and use as party favors.

MAKES: Makes 2 cups of face paint

INGREDIENTS:
½ cup cold cream (like Noxzema or Pond's)
1 cup cornstarch
½ cup water
food coloring
extra fine glitter

DIRECTIONS: Using a whisk, mix together the cream and cornstarch in bowl until smooth. Whisk in a little water at a time so that it gets easily absorbed.

Divide the concoction into several small bowls and add a few drops of food coloring to each one. Whisk each mixture until the color is completely mixed in. Then put into small containers with lids so the paint will last for up to two weeks.

Flower Perfume

ne way to capture the beautiful smells of summer is to make your very own flower perfume. Although it is not very hard to do, it does require some boiling water, so you will need a grown-up on hand.

YOU WILL NEED: flowers, cheesecloth, a pot, and water

Step 1: Gather the most fragrant flowers in your garden. You will need at least 2 cups of flowers.

Step 2: Place cheesecloth over a sturdy pot. Place your flower collection on top of the cheesecloth and cover with water. Let the flowers sit overnight and through the next day.

Step 3: Gather the cheesecloth with the flowers inside into a bundle and squeeze any extra water out into the pot of water.

Step 4: Put the pot of flower water over medium heat and let the water boil until you only have a few teaspoons left. This will be your perfume! Pour it very carefully into a small glass jar and save for very special occasions.

COMBINATIONS OF SCENTS TO ATTRACT THE FAIRIES:

- ⚙ Pine: To awaken the fairies

- ⚙ Lavender: To calm the fairies

- ⚙ Peonies: To allow you to dream of fairies

MUD PIES

Few things in the wonderful world of mud capture the imagination as much as a mud pie. Perhaps because you are combining two of the best words in a kid's vocabulary—mud and pie. The beauty of mud pie making is that it can start simply and be added to over time with elaborate recipes and kitchen set ups. But to start all you really need is a good patch of dirt, some water, and some meal ideas—pies, pizza, tacos, muffins, soup. Ask your parents if they have any old kitchen items— empty spice jars, mason jars, rusted

muffin tins. Recyclable containers, such as the bottoms of old milk jugs and plastic salad containers, work wonders with mud cooking.

Remember that word *instinctive*, meaning you were born to do this, well, mud pies, my friend, are every child's birth right. And I have to tell you that some of my favorite dining experiences ever were when my children served me at their mud cafes. Menus were passed out with such items as mud puddle soup, grilled mud sandwiches, grass gumbo, mud loaf, and mud pies á la mode for dessert. Delicious!

If, when you get started, you are hungry for other ideas, you need to check out *Mud Pies and Other Recipes* by Marjorie Winslow. This book is an outdoors cook-book. As she so wisely advises for your mud pie kitchen, "You can use a tree stump for a counter. The sea makes a nice sink; so does a puddle at the end of a hose. For a stove there is the sun, or a flat stone. And ovens are everywhere. You'll find them under bushes, in sandboxes or behind trees."

Notes...
- Boiled Buttons
- Mud puddle soup
- Grass stew
  Salads
- Tossed grass
  Sandwitchs
- Bark sandwitch
- Grilled mud sandwitch
  Main Dishes
- Fried water
- Roast rocks
- Gravel en casserole
- Mud Ball's villa
- grass gumbo
- Mud loaf

Boiled Buttons

This is a hot soup that is simple but simply delicious. Place a handful of buttons in a saucepan half filled with water. Add a pinch of white sand and dust, 2 fruit tree leaves and a blade of grass for each button. Simmer on a hot rock for a few minutes to bring out the flavor. Ladle into bowls.

Bark Sandwich

Make a buttery mix of dirt, lake water and pine needles. Heap this on a piece of birch bark and serve.

Backyard Stew

Mark off a big square in your backyard by walking 8 giant steps in each direction. Into a large stewpot put anything you find in this square such as grass, leaves, stones, twigs, berries, flowers, weeds, and so forth. Season generously with white sand and dust, and add puddle water to cover. The longer this dish stews the better it is. Recipes from *Mud Pies and Other Recipes* by Marjorie Winslow.

Fairy Soup

fairy soup is very similar to backyard stew but you make it with the fairies in mind and add a few more flowers. Often when making fairy soup, it is nice to have someone read a fairy tale or create a fairy story of your own. For some reason, fairy soup goes really well with story creation. This recipe was created by friends from Sweet Tree Art Camp.

INGREDIENTS: Lilies, roots, Queen Anne's Lace, bark, leaves, grass, stones, sticks, pine fronds, weeds

DIRECTIONS: Stir really well and leave in the sun to cook for 20 minutes.

Troll Soup

ot everyone likes to make fairy soup. Sometimes it is fun to work with the fairies' less popular cousins and give them a little snack. This soup was also created by friends from Sweet Tree Art Camp.

"The first step is to add water from the hose. Then add bark, pine cones, lots of leaves so it gets really thick, little flowers, sticks, grass, started with a stone but took it out. Let sit on a stump until everything was cooked."

Eve Bunting wrote a magical book called The Night Tree about a family who every year before Christmas head to the woods to decorate a tree with food for the animals. They cover this tree with berries, birdseed, carrots and apples. It is their way of celebrating the holidays with nature and giving back to the animals around them. Creating your own night tree celebration is not only a great family activity but it can help the animals in winter.

First, find a tree in your backyard or deep in the woods nearby. You can create lots of animal friendly decorations like strings of cheerios, dried apples, carrots with holes hammered in the tops to thread string through, and birdseed cookies. After you have hung up your ornaments, come back to see if the animals have eaten anything and look for tracks around your tree. The following recipes are for the animals and birds to enjoy.

Birdseed Cookies

emember what I said earlier, if the birds are happy, then the fairies are happy. Here is a great cookie recipe for the birds and the animals. You can make a bunch of these and hang them from a tree. Notice the footprints that come to this tree and you will get an idea of how many different types of animals enjoyed your cookies!

DIRECTIONS: In a small sauce pan, mix one packet of pectin with two cups of water and bring to a boil, stirring frequently.

In a large bowl, mix one cup of flour with three cups of birdseed. Add liquid mixture and stir.

Fill mini muffin tins with mixture, or form balls by hand. Cut straws into two-inch pieces and then poke into the center of the cookie. This will allow a hole to set in the cookies so you can string a piece of yarn later.

Let the cookies set for about six hours before removing them from the muffin tray. Depending on how dry they are when you pull them out, you might need to turn them upside down and allow them to set in the bottoms as well.

Tie a string or piece of yarn through the hole and hang them on a tree for our animal friends to enjoy.

Cranberry Bird Popsicles

right red cranberries and crystal clear ice, make for beautiful winter bird feeders. They are easy to do but they do work best with an actual popsicle maker. Instead of using a popsicle stick though, you stick a loop of yarn into the water before it freezes.

DIRECTIONS: Drop about five cranberries in each popsicle cavity. Fill about ¾ up with water. Insert loop of yarn and then freeze. Once frozen, carefully remove without pulling on the yarn, and hang on a tree.

RESOURCES

There are lots of great cook books for kids of all ages. If you are seriously interested in a cooking hobby, I suggest you check out your local library and read as many of them as you can. Here is a list of a few cookbooks that I referred to while writing this book as well as a few that I have used over and over through-out my life as a cook.

Barefoot Contessa by Ina Garten

Chop Chop: The Kids Guide to Cooking Real Food with Your Family by Sally Sampson

Cooking Rocks: Rachael Ray's 30-Minute Meals for Kids by Rachael Ray

Cooking with Children 15 Lessons for Children 7 and Up Who Really Want to Learn How to Cook by Marion Cunningham

Fairies Cookbook by Barbara Beery

Fairy Tale Feasts: A Literary Cookbook for Young Readers and Eaters by Jane Yolen and Heidi E.Y. Stemple

The Forest Feast for Kids by Erin Gleeson

Honest Pretzels and 64 Other Amazing Recipes for Cooks Ages 8 & Up by Mollie Katzen

How to Cook Everything by Mark Bittman

Ice Pop Joy by Anni Daulter

Let's Have a Tea Party! Special Celebrations for Little Girls by Emilie Barnes

Mermaid Cookbook by Barbara Beery

Pink Princess Cookbook by Barbara Beery

Smitten Kitchen: Recipes and Wisdom from an Obsessive Home Cook by Deb Perelman

Taking Tea with Alice by Dawn Hylton Gottlieb and Diane Sedo

The Ultimate Step-By-Step Kid's First Cookbook by Nancy McDougall and William Lingwood

WEBSITES

Just as there are hundreds of good books on cooking, there are thousands of good websites dedicated to cooking. This is a very short list of a few of the ones I checked out and others that are dedicated just to kids cooking.

Allrecipes.com

Chopchopmag.org

Cookingwithkids.org

Cookingwithmykid.com

Foodnetwork.com (cooking with kids section)

Spattulatta.com

Twopeasandtheirpod.com

Weelicious.com

ACKNOWLEDGMENTS

I remember the smell of my grandmother's applesauce cake filling up her kitchen and I remember thinking she was a little bit magical. I'm not sure if it was her influence but I have always loved to bake. In fact, I was a professional baker after college for several years. The smell of the bakery and the satisfaction of turning a mix of things into delicious baked goods has stayed with me over the years as I bake for my family. But I never dreamed I would someday write a cookbook about food inspired by fairies!

Writing this book was a great metaphor for cooking, a smidge of this, a dash of that, let the book rest, mix things up and wait. Some parts worked and others didn't but in the end, a meal was created with lots of parts and pieces.

It turns out writing a cookbook is different than any other book I have written. Lots of recipes were tested over and over. My kids made things. I asked friends to try things. I had groups of kids creating recipes and tasting.

I could not have done this alone. It would've been like cooking without gas.

Thank you first to Michael Steere for suggesting this idea. Lynda Chilton for her recipes, design skills and endless patience. Margaret Milnes, Sharon Kunz, and Shana Capozza are the real marketing magicians. Thank you to the kids who helped pose, cook, and taste: Bennett, Ava, Matilda, Cora, Graham, Amelia, Marguerite, Luke, Brian, and Charlie. And to their parents who put up with sugar overload.

But the lion share of the cooking and tasting was conducted by my tireless, sweet-toothed daughters and husband. Thank you, Daphne for making so many of these recipes and for all the great suggestions with each one. Phoebe, thank you for taking so many photographs and for teaching me how to display food in a striking way. And Jeff, thank you for always cleaning up our messes!

Also by Liza Gardner Walsh

Fairy House Handbook

Fairy Garden Handbook

Fairy Houses All Year

Where Do Fairies Go When it Snows

Do Fairies Bring the Spring

Treasure Hunters Handbook

Muddy Boots

Ghost Hunter's Handbook